Raphy and the Constellation of Lost Memories

Written by Rudy Abitbol
Illustrated by Tanya Maneki
Copyright 2023 by Rudy Abitbol

All rights reserved. This book or any portion thereof may not be reproduced or used at any manner whatsoever without the express written permission of the publisher except for the use of brief quotations in a book review.

First printing 2023

Raphy and the Constellation of Lost Memories

by Rudy Abitbol

illustrations by Tanya Maneki

Once there was a little boy named Raphy,
Whose love for his grandpa was oh, so hefty,
Together they'd play soccer by the shore,
And share stories, forever more.

But one day, grandpa started to forget,
Things he once knew, which made him upset,
Raphy didn't understand,
Why grandpa could no longer hold his hand.

He'd ask for things that weren't near,
And sometimes he'd just blankly stare,
Raphy felt lost and didn't know what to do,
So he asked his grandma, "What's happened to grandpa, please help me understand, too?"

Grandma smiled and took his hand,
And led him out to the backyard's land,
She pointed up to the dark night sky,
And said "Raphy, do you see the stars up high?"

Raphy nodded, and looked above,
As grandma continued with her tale of love,
She said "Every night, the Earth wears a cover,
An old blanket that's been here time after time.

"Just like grandpa's mind, it may be night,
But the love and memories still shine bright."
Raphy understood what grandma meant,
The message of love she had just sent.

Raphy looked up at the sky once more,
And felt a warmth deep in his core,
He knew that grandma was right,
And he'd love grandpa, day and night.

From that day on, Raphy knew,
That the love for his grandpa would always be true,
Just like the stars shining so bright,
Guiding grandpa through the darkest night.

He'd remind him of old memories,
And spark joy that flows like the sea's breeze.
Together they'd navigate this test,
With love and patience, doing their best.

And his grandpa, though his mind was hazy,
Was still the grandpa Raphy loved so amazingly,
So Raphy learned, in his own way,
That love can conquer any day.

Made in United States
North Haven, CT
24 June 2023